He … actice

shape and space
handling data

Shirley Clarke & Barry Silsby
Illustrated by Sascha Lipscomb

Notes for parents

Each activity in this book tests your child.
It will show you what your child is achieving, and advise on how you can help improve your child's performance. Do remember that your child's teacher will be able to tell you a great deal more about his or her ability.

How you can help
You can support your child in the following ways:

* make sure he/she knows what the instructions mean, reading them out or explaining them in your own words.

* encourage your child to 'try things out' if he/she feels unsure of the answer, either on scrap paper or by talking it through.

* don't put your child under pressure. The activities in this book are designed to be fun, and your child will benefit from doing, discussing and enjoying them.

* if your child gets stuck, try saying 'What do you think the answer may be?'

* always emphasise how well your child has done, particularly pointing out when he/she has got close to the right answer.

* talk to your child about the symbols at the end of each test, which help him or her to begin self-assessment. This is what they mean:

How much did you like doing this?

a lot **a bit** **not much**

How much help did you need?

a lot **a bit** **not much**

Ask your child to circle one of the three faces, and one of the three hands. Children perform best when they are enjoying what they are doing, and can do many things with help which they cannot do alone. Selecting the appropriate symbol will help you and your child to assess both these factors.

TEST 1

Shape sort

Look at these shapes. There are three different types. Choose three different coloured pencils and shade each type a different colour.

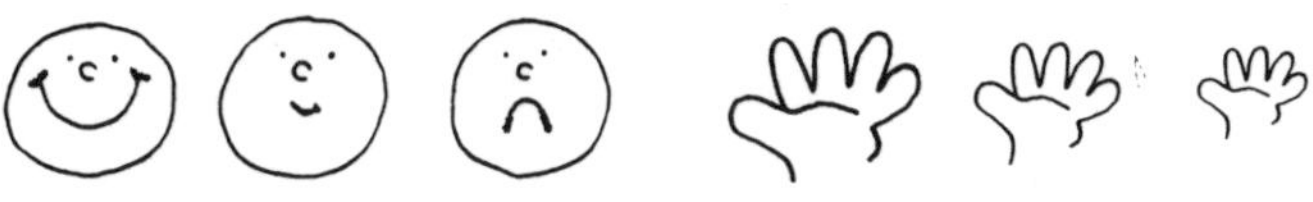

Mapping

Which of these do you like?

Join the foods you like to the  **.**

Join the foods you don't like to the  **.**

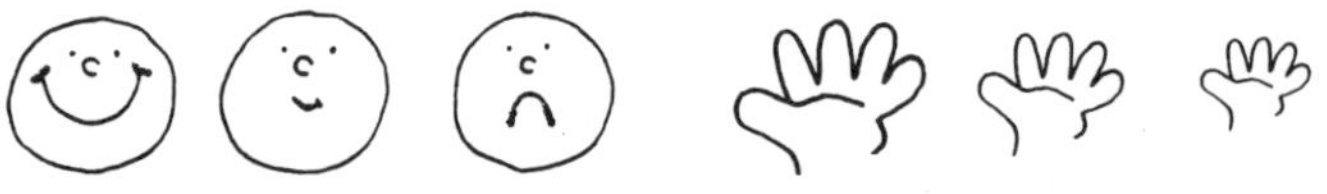

TEST 3

Where is Tabby?

Where is Tabby? Tick the right answer.

1 Tabby is...	
inside the box.	
on the box.	
behind the box.	

2 Tabby is...	
above the chair.	
on the chair.	
under the chair.	

3 Tabby is...	
behind the door.	
under the door.	
next to the door.	

4 Tabby is...	
on the table.	
above the table.	
under the table.	

5 Tabby is...	
next to the tree.	
in the tree.	
behind the tree.	

Spot the sets

Why do these things go together?

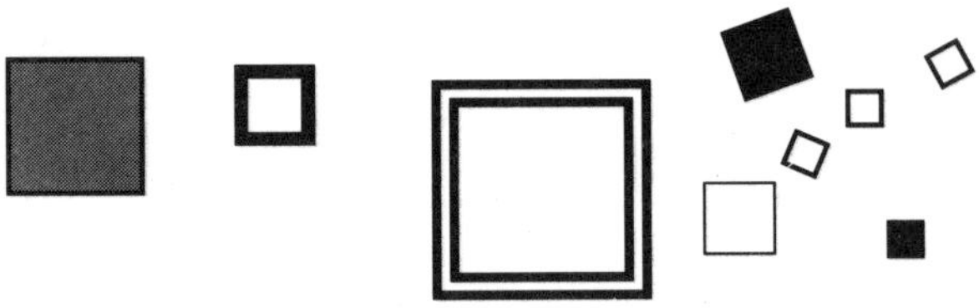

They are all ________________.

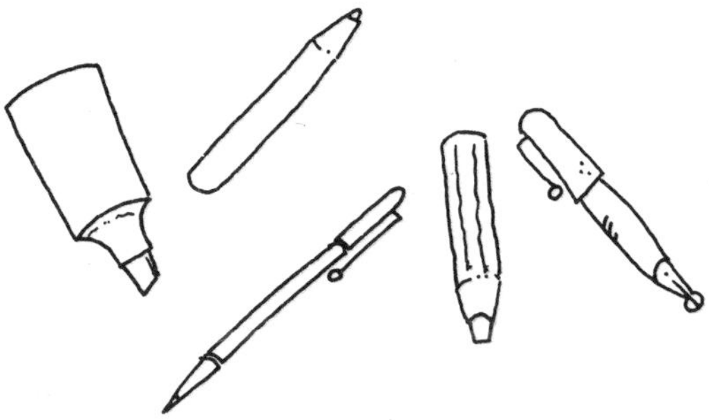

They are all ________________.

They are all ________________.

They are all ________________.

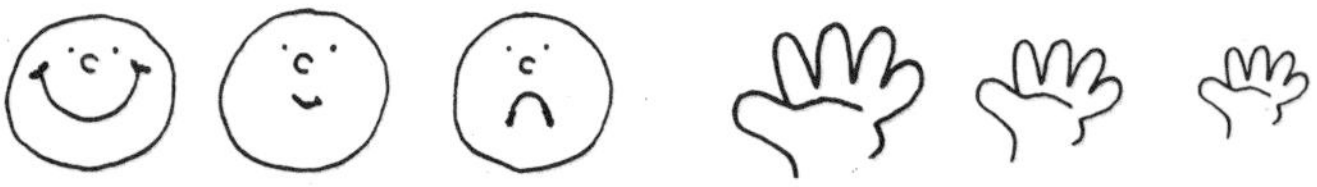

Probably

Decide whether these things <u>might happen</u>, <u>will definitely happen</u> or <u>will never happen</u>. Join them to the correct sign using different coloured pencils.

Pigs will learn to fly.

Ice-cream will be free for a day.

Someone will be born today.

I will swim two kilometres.

It will rain this week.

I will have children when I grow up..

Flowers will talk.

The sun will set this evening.

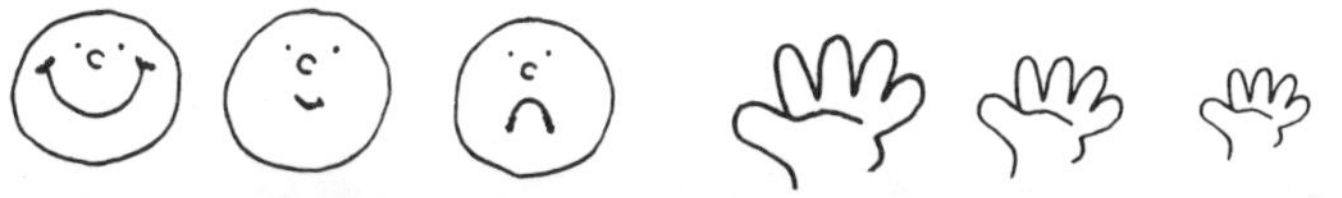

TEST 10

Survey

Ask your family or friends what their favourite drink is. Fill in the chart below.

NAME	coke	lemonade	orange juice	coffee	tea	water

Now fill in the chart below using what you have found out.

Tally (𝍸 = 5) or tick in the first column and write the total in the last column.

Drink	People who like it	Total
coke		
lemonade		
orange juice		
coffee		
tea		
water		

TEST 11

3D shapes

Join the shapes to the correct labels using different coloured pencils.

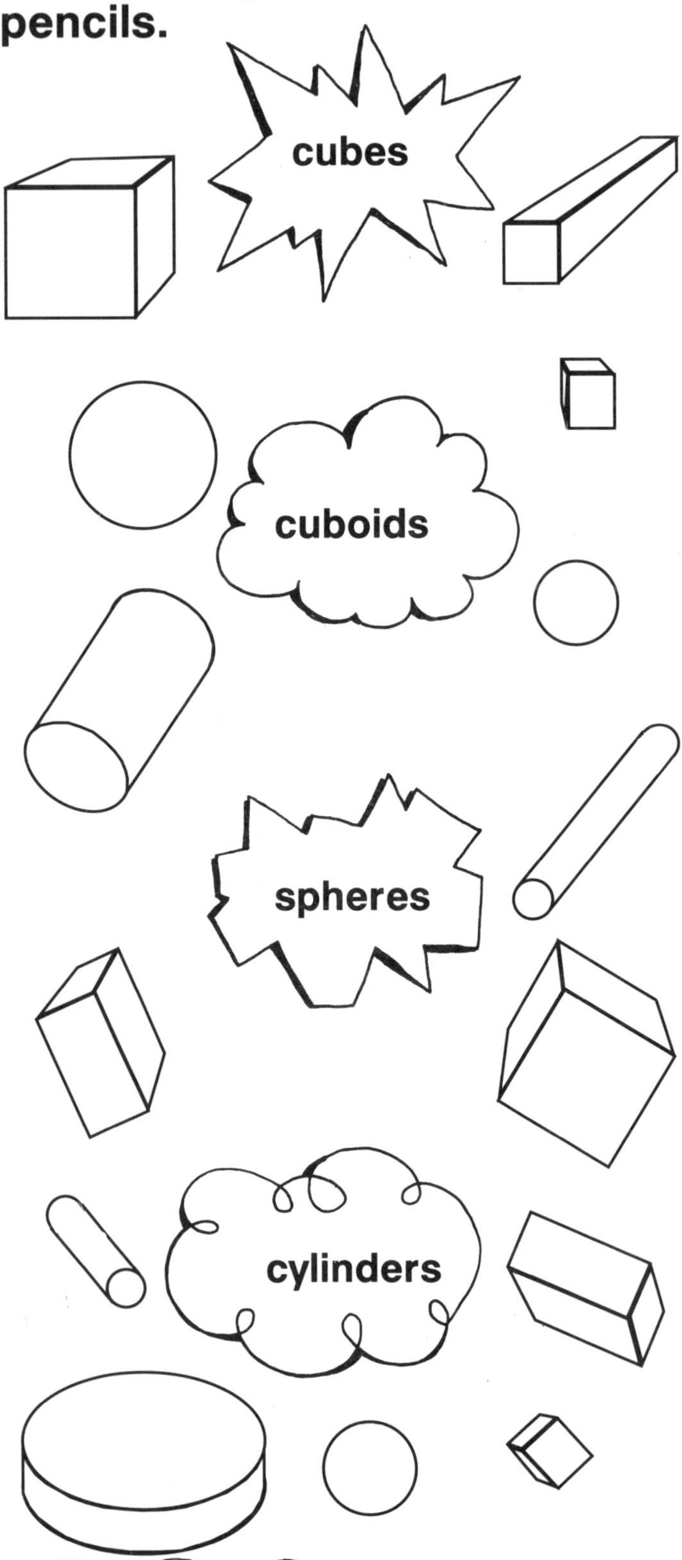

Car graph

Use the information in this chart to colour in the graph below.

Colour	Number of cars in the car park
blue	𝍸 𝍸 I
red	𝍸 𝍸 III
white	𝍸 𝍸
grey	III
gold	II
green	𝍸 III

Graph of colours of cars in car park

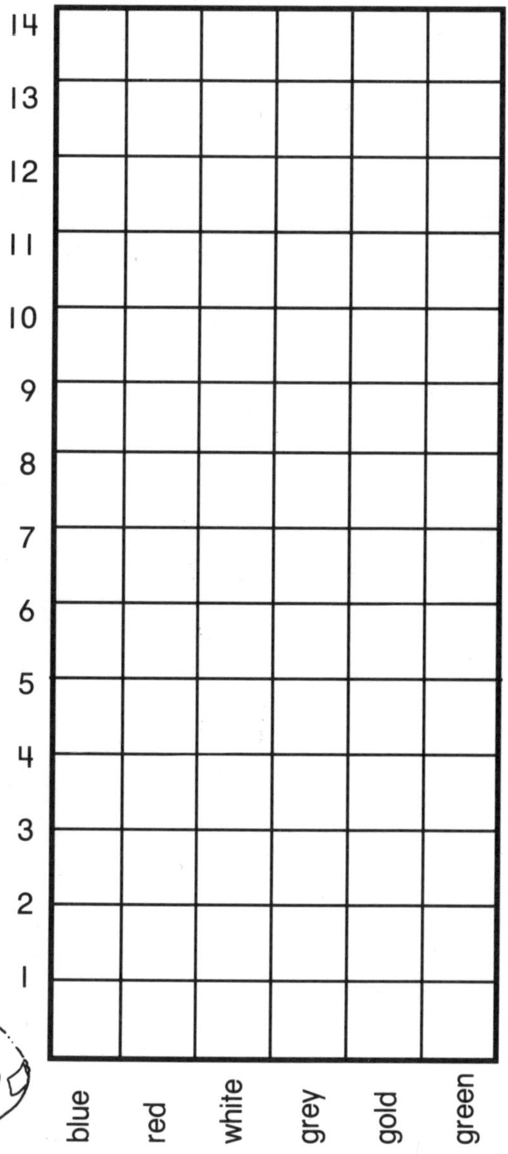

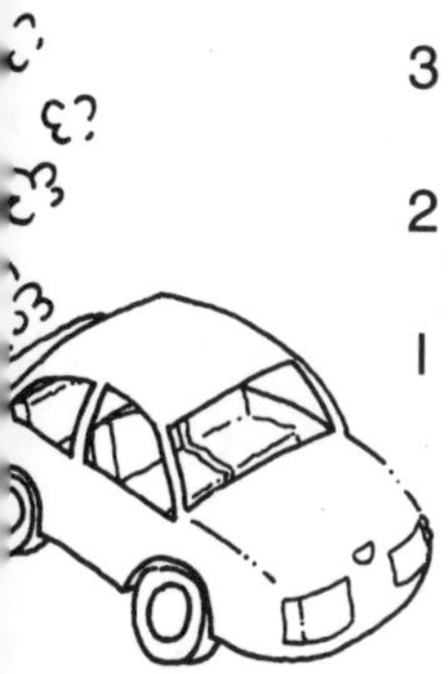

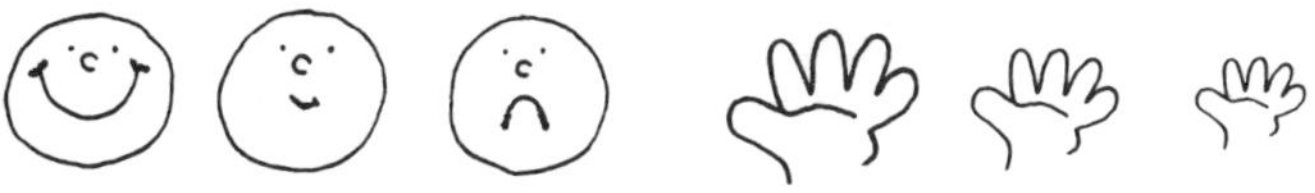

Shape properties

Join the shapes to the correct descriptions using different coloured pencils.

TEST 14

What does it tell you?

How?	Numbers of children	Total
walk	𝍸 𝍸 𝍸 |	
bus	|||	
car	𝍸 𝍸 |	
bike	||	

Anna collected information about the ways children in her class come to school. Using Anna's chart can you answer these questions?

1 How do **most** children come to school?

walk ☐ bus ☐

car ☐ bike ☐

2 How many children come by car?

16 ☐ 3 ☐

11 ☐ 2 ☐

3 Which way of travelling is **least** popular?

walk ☐ bus ☐

bike ☐ car ☐

4 Anna forgot to include herself! She walks to school. How many children walk to school now?

15 ☐ 16 ☐

17 ☐ 18 ☐

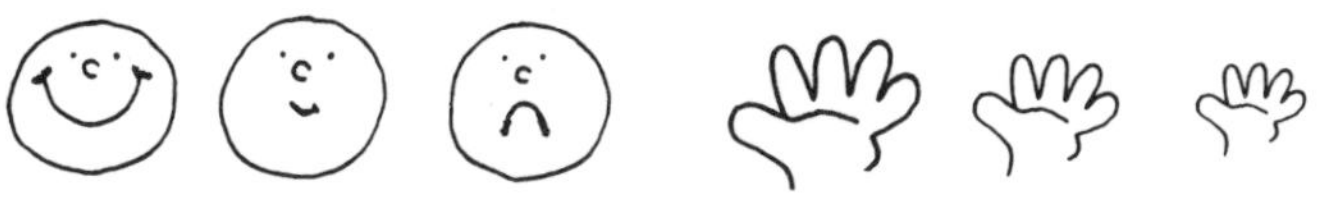

How were they sorted?

These shapes have been sorted into shapes with ____________________

and shapes with ____________________.

These shapes have been sorted into shapes with ____________________

and shapes with no ____________________.

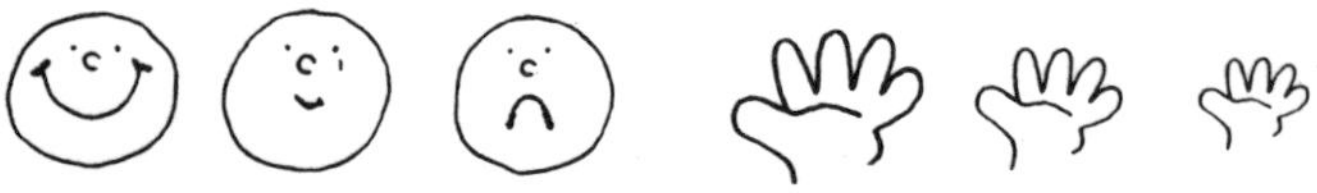

TEST 16

Symmetrical ... or not?

Tick the box to show whether these objects are symmetrical or not.

1 

symmetrical ☐

not symmetrical ☐

2 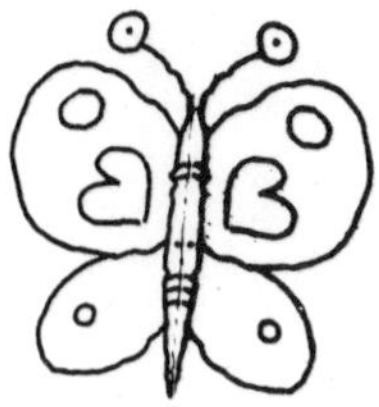

symmetrical ☐

not symmetrical ☐

3 

symmetrical ☐

not symmetrical ☐

4 

symmetrical ☐

not symmetrical ☐

5 

symmetrical ☐

not symmetrical ☐

6 

symmetrical ☐

not symmetrical ☐

TEST 17

Fill the gaps

Class sizes in Woodlea School

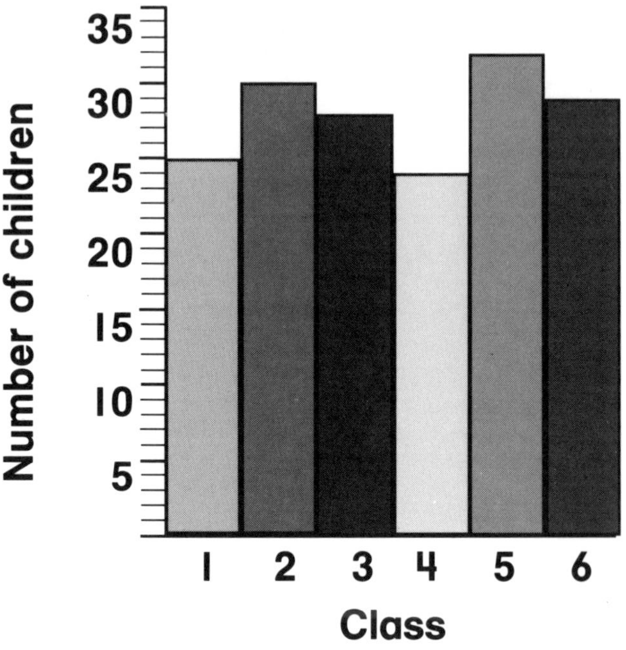

Look carefully at this graph, the fill in the missing words below.

Class _____ is the smallest class in the school.

Class 5 is the __________ class.

There are _____ children in class 3.

There are 30 children in class _____ , and _____ in class 6.

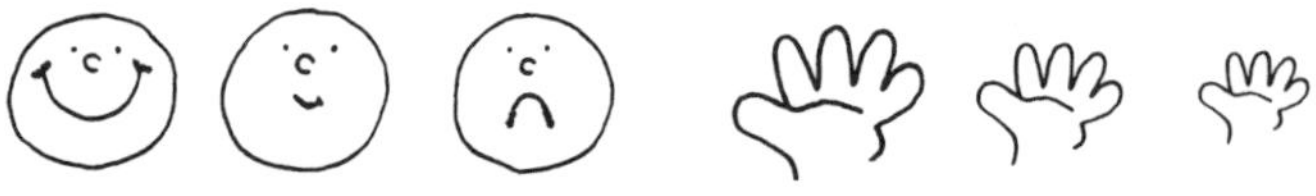

TEST 18

Follow the beetle

Use this compass to help you follow the beetle. Tick the correct directions.

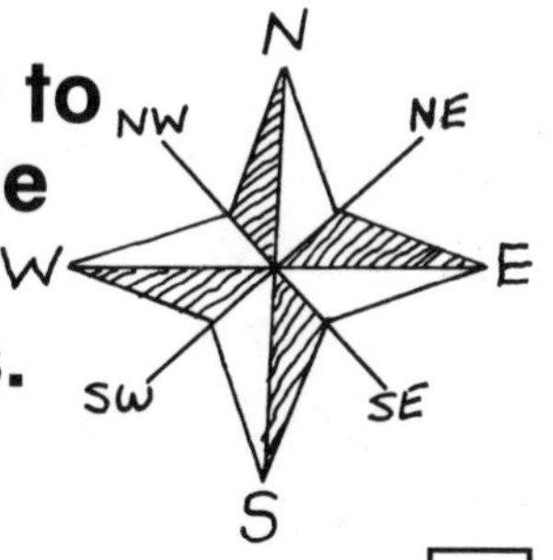

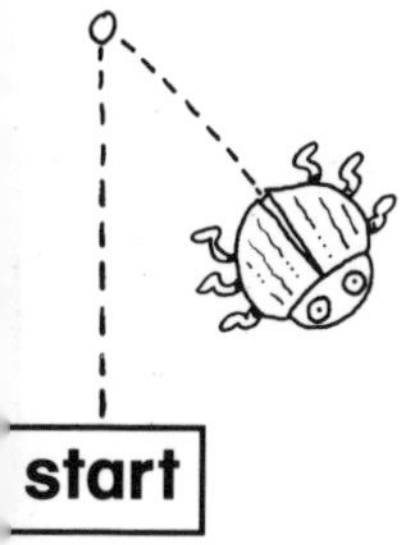

1

a North, then South East ☐

b North, then South West ☐

c South, then North ☐

d South, then South East ☐

2

a North, then West, then South ☐

b North, then East, then South ☐

c North, then West, then East ☐

d South, then East, then North ☐

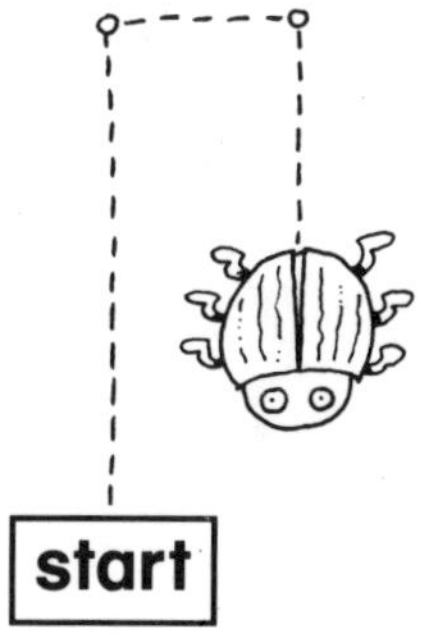

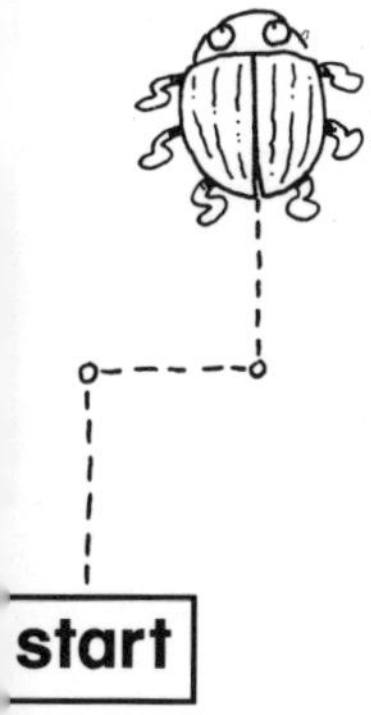

3

a North, then West, then South ☐

b North, then East, then North ☐

c North, then West, then North ☐

d North, then East, then South ☐

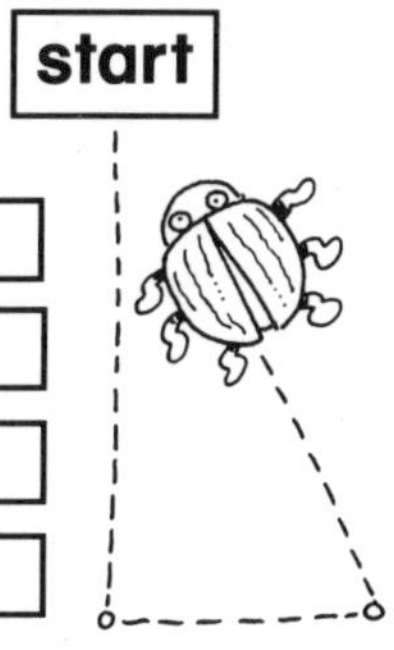

4

a North, then East, then South West ☐

b North, then East, then North West ☐

c South, then East, then North West ☐

d South, then East, then North East ☐

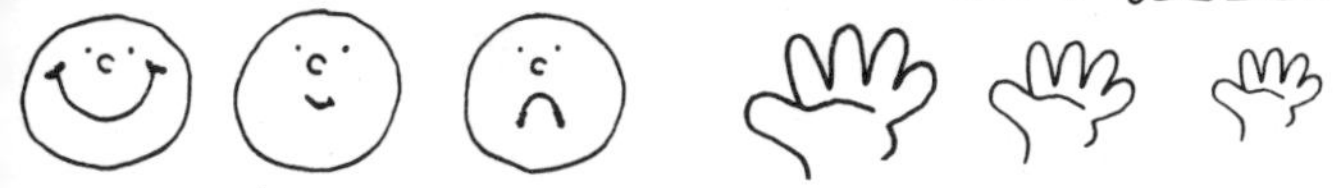

TEST 19

Turn it

Follow the directions below and draw the arrow's new position in the box. The first one has been done for you.

1  Turn clockwise $\frac{1}{2}$ of a full turn 

2  Turn anti-clockwise $\frac{1}{2}$ of a full turn

3  Turn clockwise a full turn

4  Turn anti-clockwise $\frac{1}{4}$ of a full turn

5 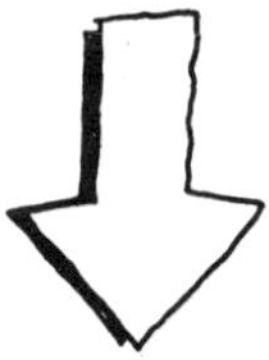 Turn clockwise $\frac{1}{4}$ of a full turn

6  Turn clockwise $\frac{1}{4}$ of a full turn

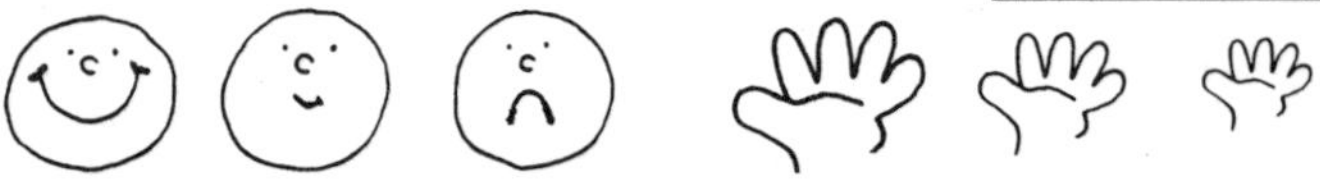

Answers
and ways to help

Test 1 Shape sort
Help by sorting and tidying in the home - socks, food, toys etc.

Test 2 Mapping
Help by talking about the food and helping your child to make decisions.

Test 3 Where is Tabby?
1 inside **2** on **3** behind **4** under **5** in
Help by using positional words when talking to your child.

Test 4 Spot the sets
1 square items **2** pens or things to write with
3 buttons **4** fruits
Help by talking about things that go together in the home and in shops.

Test 5 Seasonal mapping
Help by talking about different occasions in winter and summer, which will remind your child of appropriate clothes.

Test 6 Tabby facts
1 shortest **2** fattest **3** longer **4** longest
Help by using appropriate language when comparing objects, animals and people.

Test 7 2D shapes
The square is a rectangle/ a pentagon is any five sided shape, a hexagon is any 6 sided shape.
Help by naming shapes in the home and outside.

Test 8 Spot the right angles
1 No **2** Yes **3** Yes **4** No **5** Yes **6** No
Help by spotting right angles on corners of tables, books etc. Use the corner of this book to check.

Test 9 Probably
Help by talking about certainty, probable events and impossibilities..

Test 10 Survey
Help by making sure your child knows what the drinks are and by being available to question. Explain tallying if this is not known (~~||||~~ - the fifth count crosses through the other four).

Test 11 3D shapes
joins the shapes to the correct label:
( **cubes,**  **cuboid,**  **sphere** 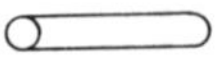 **cylinder)**

Help by pointing out shapes inside and outside the home.

Test 12 Car graph
Help by working through the task with your child. Conduct your own car colour survey to reinforce the task.

Test 13 Shape properties
Help by talking about the shapes. Look at letters of the alphabet which can be sorted in the same.

Test 14 What does it tell you?
1 walk **2** 11 **3** bike **4** 17
Help by reading the questions to your child. Talk about children's methods of transport in your child's class.

Test 15 How were they sorted?
1 straight sides and curved sides **2** right angles and no right angles
Help by drawing other sorted shapes on scrap paper and talking about them.

Test 16 Symmetrical or not?
1 Yes **2** Yes **3** No **4** Yes (line of symmetry does not have to be vertical) **5** No (because of numbers on the face) **6** No
Help by spotting symmetry in the home and in nature.

Test 17 Fill the gaps
Class 4 is the smallest. Class 5 is the biggest. There are 28 children in class 3. There are 30 children in class 2 , and 29 in class 6.
Help by reading out the text and helping to count the spaces, using a ruler across if necessary.

Test 18 Follow the beetle
1 a **2** b **3** b **4** c
Help by using the compass. Get your child to pretend to be the beetle and issue directional instructions for him/her to follow. Talk about compass directions in general, for example - the sun rises in the East and sets in the West.

Test 19 Turn it
2 ↑ **3** ↑ **4** ← **5** ← **6** ↓
Help by providing a paper arrow, which your child can physically move. Talk about clockwise and anti-clockwise.